STOP

NETWORKING

START

CONNECTWORKING®

STOP NETWORKING

START CONNECTWORKING®

Building Real Connection in a Transactional World

Jen Fort

Copyright© 2026 by Jen Fort

All rights reserved. No part of this publication may be reproduced, stored in a retrieval system, distributed, or transmitted in any form or by any means without written permission of the author, except in the case of brief quotations used in reviews or articles.

For permission, contact:
JAC Your Life LLC
www.iamjenfort.com

This book is available at special discount for bulk purchases in the United States by corporations, institutions and other organizations. For more information, please contact Jen Fort at iamjenfort@gmail.com.

Disclaimer

This book was created with the assistance of various resources, including AI as a brainstorming tool to help organize ideas and enhance clarity. However, all insights, concepts, and creative content are entirely the author's.

Trademark Notice

Wisdom & Warnings® and **Connectworking®** are registered trademarks of Jen Fort, JAC Your Life LLC. All rights reserved. Unauthorized use is strictly prohibited.

LinkedIn® is a registered trademark of LinkedIn Corporation.

This book is an independent work and is not affiliated with, endorsed by, authorized by, or sponsored by LinkedIn Corporation.

Printed in the United States of America.
First Edition: 2026

ISBN (print): 979-8-9915331-6-4

Cover design by: Margaret Cogswell
Edited by: Mark Nyman

Dedication

For every person who ever dreaded "networking."
You were never the problem;
the process was.

Author's Note

This book is not about networking. It's about being human... in conference rooms, inboxes, and everyday life. The people you'll meet in these pages are real, though their names and some details have been changed for privacy. Each story holds a similar truth: when we show up with curiosity and kindness, connection takes care of itself.

Other books by Jen Fort

365 Days of Wisdom & Warnings® book series available on Amazon:

The Badass Woman

Because You Care

Tips from the Quad

Let Them Fly

Happily Ever After

Divorce Mess to Happiness

The Wisdom & Warnings series is growing. Check out the current list using the QR code below.

Good things happen when people **talk**

Contents

Traditional Networking is Outdated 1
My Story 7
How to Use This Book 11
Chapter 1: The Power of Real 15
Chapter 2: Be Curious, Not Calculated 21
Chapter 3: Connect Before You Need To 27
Chapter 4: The Quiet Power of Showing Up 33
Chapter 5: The Art of Follow-Through 39
Chapter 6: The Confidence Loop 45
Chapter 7: From Contacts to Community 51
Chapter 8: Generosity Is Your Growth Strategy 57
Chapter 9: Kindness as a Competitive Advantage 63
Chapter 10: Connection in the Digital Age 69
Chapter 11: The Quiet Connector 75
Chapter 12: When It Doesn't Click 81
Chapter 13: The Ripple Effect 87
Chapter 14: The Human Advantage in an AI World 93
The Moment You Know It's Working 101
Bonus: Conversation Prompts 106
Bonus: 30-Day Connectworking Practice 111

Welcome
to a new way to
connect

Traditional Networking is Outdated

Why does traditional networking feel fake, and what to do instead.

If you've ever stood at a networking event clutching a drink, scanning the room for someone who isn't avoiding eye contact, and thinking, "What am I doing here?", you're not alone.

Most of us were taught that networking is the secret to career success.
We were told to *work the room, collect contacts, put ourselves out there, and follow up aggressively.*

And maybe that worked for some people; the ones who can walk into any room and charm a crowd without saying a word.

But for most of us, it feels fake.
It feels forced.
And it drains the very energy we need to build real relationships.

So, let's say it out loud: **networking, as we've known it, is dead.**
And that's something to celebrate.

The truth is, you don't need more contacts, you need connection.
Not the kind that ends with a handshake and a business card you'll never look at again, but the kind that feels like, "I see you. I get you. I'd like to stay in touch."

That's the difference between **networking** and **Connectworking**.

Networking is about collecting.
Connectworking is about connecting.

Networking is strategy.
Connectworking is sincerity.

Traditional Networking is Outdated

Networking happens out of fear... "I need something."
Connectworking happens out of curiosity... "I'd like to know or share something."

One is transactional. The other is transformational.

When I started coaching clients through layoffs and career pivots, I saw the same pattern over and over. People weren't struggling because they didn't know how to write a résumé or polish a LinkedIn profile. They were struggling because they felt *alone*.

They wanted to connect, but they didn't know how to do it without feeling awkward, salesy, or self-promotional.
So, they avoided it and made themselves feel even more isolated.

And the vicious cycle continued.

The problem wasn't confidence. It was the old model of networking itself.
It told us to focus on outcomes instead of people.
To lead with need instead of humanity.

To treat relationships like transactions instead of conversations.

And that model is finally collapsing under its own weight.

Here's what's taking its place: *a quieter, kinder, more human way of connecting.*

You don't need an elevator pitch or sales talk.
You don't need to pretend to be an extrovert.
You don't even need a perfect plan.

You just need to show up as yourself and stay curious.

When you do, the right people find you.
Not because you chased them, but because your authenticity stands out in a world full of polish and performance.

That's what this book is about.
It's about unlearning the old rules of networking and replacing them with connection that actually feels good. The kind of connection that leads to real relationships, confidence, and opportunities.

Traditional Networking is Outdated

You'll meet people in these pages who didn't find their next job through job boards or cold emails, but through genuine conversations; on dog walks, in coffee shops, and in messages sent without expectation.
They didn't network harder. They *connected better.*

You'll also find practical steps, reflection prompts, and 30 days of small actions to help you practice Connectworking your way — especially if you've been out of work, out of practice, or just plain burned out.

No scripts. No rules. No name tags.

Just real humans helping each other move forward.

So, take a deep breath.
Put away the elevator pitch.
And get ready to remember something simple and powerful:

You don't need to impress people to connect with them.
You just need to be yourself.

Sometimes **unplanned** becomes the **next step**

My Story

The Moment Everything Changed

A few years ago, I found myself on the losing end of what I call an "unexpected departure."
In plain English: I got laid off.

After almost twenty years with the same company, I was suddenly packing up my desk, handing in my badge, and wondering who I was without a title or a team.

The first few weeks, I did what most people do, I licked my wounds. I walked a lot. I reflected. I stared at my LinkedIn profile wondering how to sum up two decades of experience in a few neat lines. And somewhere between frustration and freedom, I decided to take a 180-degree pivot into something completely new.

I became a **career transition coach**.

Like Barb, the coach who helped me through my own career transition, now I help other people navigate the same emotional rollercoaster.

Since then, I've worked with thousands of people in transition — executives, analysts, teachers, scientists, and creatives — all figuring out how to turn their *Oh No!* into *Heck Yes!*

Every story is different, but the patterns are surprisingly familiar.

People don't get stuck because they lack talent or ambition.
They get stuck because of how they *see* connection.

When I ask clients to tell me about their networking efforts, I often get the same response:

"I reached out to a bunch of people, and nothing happened, so I stopped."

It's the classic transaction mindset: one message, one ask, one shot, and if it doesn't produce the desired result, we declare, "Networking doesn't work."

My Story

But that's not connection; that's a vending machine.

Real connection isn't about simply asking for favors; it's about curiosity, generosity, and humanity.
Real connection involves approaching people with the simple desire to *learn* and *share*, not to *leverage*.

The shift from "What can I get?" to "What can I give?" changes everything.

This book was born from that realization.
I wanted to rewrite the rules of networking to make them human again for both introverts and extroverts, for the college graduate to the seasoned executive, as well as the person starting over mid-career, like me.

What you'll find here are stories, examples, and easy-to-apply practices that will help you connect in a way that feels natural, not forced.
Connection shouldn't feel like a chore. Instead, it can feel as natural as breathing.

Whether you're rebuilding after a layoff, growing your career, or simply wanting to meet people in a more meaningful way, this book is your permission slip to drop the pitch and bring your whole self to the conversation.

That's what Connectworking is all about — bringing back the *human* in human connection.

How to Use This Book

Connection is a practice,

not a performance.

This isn't a book you just read once and shelve. It's a book you live with.

Connectworking isn't about mastering a skill; it's about shifting how you see and engage with people. The more you practice, the more natural it becomes. You'll start to notice patterns, sparks, and opportunities that were always there, you just weren't tuned into them yet.

Read at your own pace.

Each chapter stands on its own, but they also build on one another.
You can read straight through or jump to the section that fits what you need most in the moment, whether

that's confidence, generosity, or how to recover when a connection goes quiet.

If you're short on time, pick one chapter each week and apply one practice.
Connection isn't a sprint. It's a new way of being.

Try the exercises

Throughout the book, you'll find short reflections, challenges, and "Try This" moments.
They aren't homework, they're conversation starters between you and yourself.
Take a few minutes to actually do them.
They're where the real growth happens.

Use the 30-Day Connectworking Plan

At the end of the book, you'll find a simple month-long roadmap containing 30 days of small, intentional actions designed to help you strengthen your connection habits.
Think of it as training for your *human muscle*.

Most of the activities take less than ten minutes a day.

How to Use this Book

By the end of those 30 days, you'll have built momentum and confidence that naturally carries forward.

Make it yours.

Some people will read this book quietly and reflectively. Others will highlight, underline, and share it with friends.
There's no wrong way to use it.

Whether you're an introvert, extrovert, or somewhere in between, *Connectworking* meets you where you are. It's less about changing who you are and more about reclaiming what's already true: humans were born to connect.

Grab a pen, a notebook, or an unemployed friend.
Circle the ideas that feel right.
Ignore the ones that don't.
And keep practicing one conversation, moment, and connection at a time.

Because this isn't just a book.
It's a new way of being in the world.

STOP NETWORKING... START CONNECTWORKING®

Authentic
is
magnetic

Chapter 1

The Power of Real

Drop the polish. Pick up authenticity.

If you've been laid off recently, you already know how strange it feels to be "out there" again.

You wake up with nowhere to be and everyone's advice echoing in your head:

"Hit up your LinkedIn contacts."

"Work your network."

"Don't you know someone at MicroSafe? Call them!"

You try, but it all feels awkward.

The coffee chats feel forced.

The networking events feel like speed dating with business cards.

And the more you try to sound confident, the less like *yourself* you sound.

Most of us were taught to network like we were performing on stage: polish the story, perfect the smile, and be sure to hit every talking point. But here's the truth: people don't connect with polish. They connect with *authenticity* and *presence*.

> **Real isn't loud. It's simply honest.**

Let me tell you about a client who proved that beautifully.

Fred had been laid off after thirteen years in a corporate role. The shock was still fresh.

One morning, he took his dog for a walk, mostly to clear his head, and ran into a neighbor walking her dog. While the dogs seemed to know each other, he and his neighbor lived on the same street for years but had never met.

Trying to make small talk, he laughed and said, "Wow, my dog's getting so much exercise since I got laid off."

That single line changed everything.

The Power of Real

She smiled. "You too? I was laid off last year, but I recently ended up somewhere much better."
And just like that, two strangers connected; talking about layoffs, uncertainty, and the possibility for new beginnings.

A few weeks later, that same neighbor stopped by to say her new company was hiring.
By the end of the month, Fred had a new job.

Not because he had a perfect elevator pitch.
Not because he networked strategically.
But because he was honest and real in an ordinary moment.

That's what *Connectworking* is about.
It's not the art of sounding impressive.
It's the practice of being authentic.

Real conversation. Real curiosity. Real kindness.

You don't need to memorize scripts or chase handshakes.
You just need to show up fully human and let people see the person behind the résumé.

Because people don't hire résumés.

They hire trust.

And trust starts with truth.

Try This: The Real Test

Before your next professional or personal conversation, pause and ask yourself:

- Am I trying to impress or connect?

- Am I speaking like a person or like a profile?

- What would I say if this were a friend, not a contact?

You don't need the right words.

You just need the real ones.

Connectworking Challenge

Today, say something genuine to a colleague, a neighbor, or even a stranger.
Skip the small talk and say what's true.

> Ask a question.

> Pay a compliment.

> Comment on a shared experience.

You might be surprised how often "real" opens doors that polish never could.

Next up: Be Curious, Not Calculated: Curiosity opens doors that strategy can't.

Curiosity beats clever every time

Chapter 2

Be Curious, Not Calculated

Curiosity opens doors that strategy can't.

Somewhere along the way, "networking" became a game of angles.

- Who do you know?
- Who do *they* know?
- What can they do for you?
- How can you say the right thing to get what you want?

It's exhausting.
And it's exactly why so many people avoid networking altogether.

When you approach people with an ulterior motive, they feel it.

The polished tone and rehearsed enthusiasm. The subtle *ask* hiding behind small talk.

We think we're being professional. But what we're really doing is *protecting ourselves* from rejection or looking needy.

And that's what kills connection faster than anything else.

> **Curiosity turns awkward into easy.**

Curiosity, on the other hand, disarms people. It opens space. It says, *I'm interested in you,* not *I'm trying to get something from you.*

Let me share with you a recent coaching session. Robert was frustrated and tired of reaching out to former coworkers who never replied.

So, I asked him to forget strategy for a minute and focus on curiosity instead.

"Can you find a friend or former colleague you have lost touch with?" I asked. "Not someone who can hire

Be Curious, Not Calculated

you, just someone you'd love to hear or learn from. Ask them one question… something real."

A few days later, he messaged a manager he had fallen out of touch with but followed on LinkedIn.
He didn't ask for a job.
He asked, "How did you stay motivated when your company went through layoffs last year?"

That one question turned into a 30-minute conversation.
That conversation turned into a renewed mentorship.
A few months later, when her team had an opening, she called him.

Curiosity did what calculation never could.

When you're curious, you don't have to perform.

You just show up as a learner: open, humble, and engaged.
People feel safe with that energy and want to help because we are wired to respond to genuine interest.

We like being seen. We like being asked about our path, our opinions, our perspectives.

Curiosity is the simplest way to give someone that gift.

And when you do, something amazing happens... you become memorable.
Not because you were impressive.
But because you were *interested*.

Try This: The Curiosity Loop

Next time you talk with someone new, try this simple pattern:

Ask > Listen > Reflect > Follow Up

1. **Ask**: A real question, not a scripted one. "What's been the most surprising part of your job lately?"

2. **Listen**: Not for your turn to talk, but for what they care about.

3. **Reflect**: Show that you heard them.
   "That's a really interesting perspective; it sounds like you value [fill in the blank]."

Be Curious, Not Calculated

4. **Follow Up:** A few days later, send a quick note. "I listened to that podcast you suggested. Thank you again for sharing."

That's connection.
No tricks. No tactics. Just paying attention.

> 💬 **Connectworking Challenge**
>
> This week, reach out to one person you admire, not for a job or referral, but to simply to ask them something real.
> It could be, "What's one thing you wish you'd known before switching careers?" or "What do you love most about what you do now?"
> Then listen.
> You'll be amazed how quickly curiosity builds bridges that calculation never could.

Next up: Connect Before You Need To: The best time to build a network is before you need one.

Act with **intention** not **impulse**

Chapter 3

Connect Before You Need To

The best time to build a network is before you need one.

When people lose a job, they often reach out in a panic.

They send dozens of emails and DMs in a week, all with the same line:

"Hey, just wanted to catch up! By the way, I'm on the job market looking for a new job."

And suddenly, everyone feels like a means to an end.

I don't say that with judgment. I've been there and so have most of my clients.

When you're scared or uncertain, reaching out feels like survival.

But here's the hard truth: that's not connection; that's reactionary networking.

And it rarely works.

Think about it this way: you wouldn't plant a garden the day you want to eat fresh tomatoes. You start months earlier, planting seeds and trusting that some will grow.

> **Plant a garden before you need the veggies.**

Relationships work the same way.

When you tend to them before you need them, and water them with curiosity, check in, celebrate, and show up, they grow deep roots.
Then, when life changes (and it always does), those connections naturally support you.

That's what *Connectworking* is all about: creating habits of connection long before you're desperate for them.

One of my clients learned this the hard way. Tamara had a long, successful career at a major company until the reorganization came. Overnight, her position was in jeopardy.

She started reaching out to old coworkers, managers, vendors, and anyone who might have a job lead. But most of the messages went unanswered. Not because people didn't care, but because the relationships had gone dormant and people were busy. Years of her own busyness had pushed them into silence.

When she finally did reconnect, she realized something important:
They didn't remember what she'd been doing lately.
They didn't know what mattered to her now.
And she didn't know what was happening in their lives either.

It wasn't that her network had disappeared, it had just *stopped breathing.*

Thankfully, her job was not eliminated, but she decided to make a change.

She started reaching out when she didn't need anything.

- A quick note of encouragement to someone she saw on LinkedIn.

- A "just checking in" text to a former colleague.

- A short voice message congratulating someone on a new role.

Within months, those little acts started coming back around.

Now, she had the confidence, should she ever find herself out in the cold after a corporate reorganization, that her network would be there to help.

What changed?
The relationships were alive again.

Here's the thing: people want to help, they just don't want to feel like a transaction.
If the first time you reach out is when you need a favor, the conversation feels heavy.

But if you've already invested a little time and care, it feels natural.

The goal isn't to keep score. It's to keep connection.

Try This: The 3-3-3 Habit

Once a week, pick:

- **3 people to reconnect with** — old coworkers, friends, mentors.

- **3 people to encourage** — maybe someone posting about a new project.

- **3 people to meet** — new contacts, introductions, or people you've admired from afar.

Send a short, personal message. Something like:

- "Saw your post and it made me smile. How's life treating you lately?"

- "I thought of you on my morning run. I'm still impressed you ran the New York City marathon! How are things going?"

It doesn't need a strategy, but it does need sincerity.

> **Connectworking Challenge**
>
> This week, reach out to three people for *no specific reason at all.*
> No hidden agenda. No job lead. No "ask."
> Simply to say, "I thought of you."
>
> You might be surprised how fast warmth returns to relationships that have been waiting to hear from you.

Next up: The Quiet Power of Showing Up: How consistency, visibility, and kindness make you magnetic.

Chapter 4

The Quiet Power of Showing Up

How consistency, visibility, and kindness make you magnetic.

A funny thing happens when you lose your job. The world gets quiet and so do you.

The emails stop and the meetings vanish. The routine that used to define your days suddenly disappears. And in that silence, you start to wonder if anyone still sees you.

I specifically remember one client, Karen, whose experience was similar to my own.

She said, "It's like I fell off the radar. People I worked with for years didn't even check in."

She wasn't angry, she was stunned. She'd spent her career helping others, showing up for her team, and volunteering for every project. But when she needed connection, the phone stayed silent.

We talked about it, and I asked her a question that caught her off guard:
"Have *you* stayed visible since leaving?"

She paused. "Honestly? No. I didn't want to bother anyone. I thought I'd wait until I had something positive to share."

That's the moment most people lose touch with opportunity — not when they get laid off, but when they *disappear.*

Here's the truth: connection isn't built in grand gestures. It's built in steady, gentle presence.

Showing up, even quietly, reminds people you exist and that you care. It's not about bragging or posting daily updates; it's about staying part of the conversation in a way that feels real to you.

The Quiet Power of Showing Up

Karen took that to heart. She started small by commenting thoughtfully on former colleagues' posts, sharing an article that inspired her, sending a short note to someone who'd been laid off too.

> **Just show up... consistency beats confidence.**

No pitches or agenda. Just presence.

Two months later, her former manager reached out: "Hey, I saw your comment on LinkedIn. Can we talk?"

His team was expanding and they were hiring again.

That's the quiet power of showing up.

We live in a loud world. Everyone's shouting for attention with louder posts, stronger opinions and flashier headlines.

But people don't always remember the loudest voices. They remember the ones who consistently show up.

Consistency builds comfort. Comfort builds trust. And trust builds everything else.

When you show up regularly in person, online, or even through a kind message, you create what psychologists call *familiarity bias*. People naturally lean toward what feels familiar. In other words, when you stay visible, people think of you first, not because you demanded it, but because you were present.

That's not manipulation, it's humanity.

We gravitate toward people who make us feel safe, seen, and supported.
And that starts with simply being present.

Try This: The Visibility Audit

Grab a notebook or open a new page. Write down three answers:

- Where do I naturally show up? (LinkedIn, text messages, community events, volunteering, etc.)

- Where have I gone quiet?

- What would showing up *my way* look like this month?

The Quiet Power of Showing Up

Your visibility doesn't have to be loud, it just has to feel right for *you*.

For some, it's a thoughtful comment; for others, it's checking in with a former coworker.

It's not the medium that matters; it's the presence.

 Connectworking Challenge

This week, show up once intentionally and quietly. Comment on someone's post. Send a note to a friend. **Bonus points if you send a handwritten note through the mail. Attend an event you almost skipped.

Don't announce yourself. Just be there.

People notice consistency more than charisma. And sometimes, the quietest presence creates the loudest impact.

Next up: The Art of Follow-Through: How to stay connected without feeling pushy.

Action
makes you
memorable

Chapter 5

The Art of Follow-Through

How to stay connected without feeling pushy.

You've probably heard it a thousand times: *"Wait a week, then follow-up."*

That line has haunted job seekers and salespeople for years. It makes connection sound like a race you have to finish before someone forgets you.

But here's what most people get wrong: you don't need to **follow-up.** You need **follow-through.**

Follow-up is about *you.*
Follow-through is about *them.*

One of my clients, Mark, told me about a job interview that went well — or so he thought. The manager said she'd be in touch "soon." Weeks passed and he heard nothing but silence.

He started overthinking every detail: "Should I email her again? Should I call? I don't want to seem desperate."

I asked him what he actually wanted to say.
He replied. "I just want her to know I really connected with the team, and I can't stop thinking how we spent an entire afternoon discussing new technologies. It was invigorating."

"That's your message," I said. "Not a follow-up. A genuine, heartfelt thank-you."

He sent a short note that read:

"I just wanted to say I really enjoyed meeting you and the team. I'm still energized by the meeting, and I'd love to continue the conversation. I'm available between two and four most afternoons. Hope your

The Art of Follow-Through

week's going well and I look forward to connecting again."

That's it. No ask. No pressure. Just gratitude.

A week later she replied, not with the job on her team, but with a referral to another department that was hiring for a position that would be a better fit.

He got that one.

> **Follow-through turns connection into credibility.**

Here's the truth: *Follow-through is not a tactic. It's a mindset.*
It's how you stay connected without turning people into projects.

When you follow-through you're saying, "I meant what I said. I valued our conversation. I care beyond the outcome."

That kind of energy builds trust... and trust lasts longer than any single opportunity.

Think of the people who stand out to you. They're not the ones who send a dozen vague "checking in" messages.

They're the ones who remember your birthday, comment when you get promoted, or forward an article they know you'll love.

Those small moments don't feel like networking, they feel like friendship.

That's *follow-through*.

Try This: Three Ways to Reach Out Right

If you're not sure what to say after a conversation, the simplest way is to connect authentically.

Start with one of these:

1. A note of appreciation, big or small.

2. A quick share of something useful or thoughtful.

3. A heartfelt, personal check-in to see how they're doing.

The Art of Follow-Through

If your message doesn't fit one of those three, it's probably a "follow-up," and you can make it better by turning it into a "follow-through."

 Connectworking Challenge

This week, reach out to three people you've met recently; not to ask anything, but to appreciate them.

> Thank someone for their time.

> Send a resource they might enjoy.

> Congratulate them on something you noticed.

Make it short and sincere. Then move on.

You don't need to chase people. You just need to *remind them you mean it.*

Next up: The Confidence Loop: How self-belief, consistency, and compassion fuel connection.

Self-belief changes **everything.** Full stop.

Chapter 6

The Confidence Loop

How self-belief, consistency and compassion fuel connection.

Most people think confidence is something you either have or you don't.
You see it in others with their easy smile, firm handshake, and the calm way they speak. You assume they were born with it.

But that's not how it works.
Confidence isn't a trait. It's a loop.

It starts with **small actions**, turns into **experience**, builds **trust in yourself**, and circles back to more action.

That's it. No magic or instant transformation.
Just practice... one small loop at a time.

When you're in career transition, confidence takes a hit.
Even the most accomplished professionals start to question themselves.
You go from being the person others come to for answers... to wondering if anyone will even return your emails.

> **Believe in yourself and others will believe back.**

It's disorienting.
You start doubting your value.
And the moment that happens, connection becomes harder because you can't fake genuine energy when you're running on empty.

I see this all the time.
People pull back from conversations, skip events, hesitate to post or reach out because they "don't feel confident enough yet."
But here's the secret: **you gain confidence by doing, not by waiting.**

The Confidence Loop

One of my clients, Lisa, hadn't interviewed in 23 years.
She told me, "I'll start networking once I get my confidence back."
So we flipped it.
"What if you get your confidence *by* networking?" I asked.

She agreed to try something small — reaching out to a former colleague to ask how they were doing.
No pitch. No résumé. Just connection.

That one message turned into a friendly phone call. The call reminded her she still had valuable insights. That reminder led her to comment on an industry post, which sparked another conversation, this time with someone who would later become her new manager.

Action → experience → belief → more action
That's the loop.

When you're feeling low, confidence won't come from pep talks or positive affirmations alone.

Although I do love a good pep talk!

It comes from **evidence** — the proof that you're still capable and resourceful.

Every small act of showing up reinforces that truth.

Confidence isn't about volume or swagger.

It's quiet, grounded assurance that grows through repetition and compassion.

You don't need to be fearless. You just need to keep moving in small, kind steps.

Try This: The Loop in Action

The next time you hesitate to connect, use this three-step reset:

- **Act:** Do one small thing, such as send a message, share an idea, attend a call.

- **Acknowledge:** Pause afterward and say, "I did that."

- **Anchor:** Write down one sentence about what you learned or how you felt.

The Confidence Loop

Repeat that process three times this week. By the third loop, you'll start noticing: it's not that the fear went away — it's that you stopped letting it lead.

 Connectworking Challenge

Reach out to one person this week, even if your confidence feels shaky.
Tell them something kind, ask something curious, or simply check in.
Then, instead of critiquing yourself afterward, write down one thing that went well.

Confidence grows quietly, but it grows fast when you give it proof.

Next up: From Contacts to Community: How to turn quick connections into lasting relationships.

Confidence
+
Community
=
MOMENTUM

Chapter 7

From Contacts to Community

How to turn quick connections into lasting relationships.

There's a point in every job search when your contact list starts to look like a spreadsheet instead of a network.
Names. Titles. Companies.
You scroll through, trying to remember how you even know half of them.

That's when you realize: having contacts isn't the same as having community.

Contacts are names.
Community is people.

Contacts are what you collect.
Community is what you *cultivate.*

The truth is that you don't need hundreds of people to help you move forward. You just need a few who really see you, believe in you, and who you can show up for in return.

One of my clients, Denise, used to joke that her LinkedIn connections looked like a phonebook, "I've connected with everyone," she said, "but I don't *feel connected* to anyone."

When she was laid off, she posted about it online hoping her "network" would magically rally.
A few people commented. A few sent polite messages. But it didn't lead to much.

Then, a week later, a woman she barely knew — someone Denise had met once at a conference — reached out. "I remember how kind you were when we talked about my massive career change jumping from operations to product development. I was terrified to try something new, but you shared your experience in engineering, and you told me it would all work out. Well, it did work out better than I could have imagined," she said. "We're expanding. Would you like me to introduce you to my director?"

That introduction led to an interview.
And the interview led to a new role.

> **One shared experience can turn into an entire storyline.**

It wasn't the hundreds of contacts that changed her life.
It was one person who remembered how she made them *feel*.

That's the heart of *Connectworking*: turning transactional touchpoints into relationships built on care, not convenience.

Community happens when you give people a reason to stay connected and because you made them feel valued, not used.

It's built on small, genuine gestures over time.
It's not who you know — it's who you *keep knowing.*

Here's a simple truth: people want to belong somewhere.
And in a world that's increasingly digital and disconnected, belonging is rare.

When you take the time to check in, to make introductions, remember birthdays or career wins, you become a connector — someone who creates spaces of trust.
And people don't forget that.

You stop being "one of many" in their inbox and become "one of few" in their circle.

Try This: The Circle Exercise

Grab a sheet of paper.
Draw three circles — small, medium, and large — like a target.

- **Inner Circle:** The 5–10 people you can be fully honest with... the ones who cheer, challenge, and care.

From Contacts to Community

- **Middle Circle:** Professional peers, mentors, or collaborators who share mutual respect.

- **Outer Circle:** New or occasional connections you're still getting to know.

Now ask yourself:

- Who have I neglected in my inner circle?

- Who in the middle circle could I show more appreciation?

- Who in the outer circle might I bring a little closer?

You're not ranking people — you're tending to relationships like a garden.

Connectworking Challenge

This week, make one introduction that helps two people win.

No hidden agenda or expectation.

Just connection for connection's sake.

It's the fastest and most fulfilling way to grow your network.

Next up: Generosity Is Your Growth Strategy: Why giving freely is the smartest move you'll ever make.

Chapter 8

Generosity Is Your Growth Strategy

Why giving freely is the smartest move you'll ever make.

Most people think networking is about asking. Whether it's asking for advice, asking for introductions, or asking for opportunities.

But here's the truth: the people who build the strongest networks are the ones who *give* first.

Not because they're trying to earn points or look impressive.
But because it's who they are.

When generosity becomes your natural starting point, everything shifts.
Doors open when trust builds. People remember you,

not for what you wanted, but for how you made them feel.

I once coached a woman named Dafna who had been laid off from a leadership role after twenty plus years. She was well-connected, respected, and completely stuck.

"I've reached out to everyone I know," she said. "I'm not gaining any traction."

So, I asked, "When was the last time you reached out without asking for anything?"

She blinked, "Probably before the layoff."

We decided to change her strategy: no requests, only generosity.

She started small by sending articles to former teammates who might find them helpful, offering to make introductions for former colleagues also in transition, and sharing open roles she came across even if they didn't fit her.

A month later, her inbox looked different.
The same people who hadn't replied before were now

Generosity Is Your Growth Strategy

writing back.

One even said, "You reminded me why I liked working with you."

Two weeks later, that same person shared information about a job that had not yet been posted and offered to submit a referral.

Generosity did what persistence couldn't.

Generosity isn't a weakness; it's power with patience.

> **The more you give, the richer your connections become.**

When you give your time, encouragement, introductions, or ideas, you stand out in a world that's constantly taking.
You shift the energy from scarcity to abundance, from transaction to trust.
And when you do that often enough, people start thinking of you not as a job seeker, but as a connector.

There's a name for this in *Connectworking*:
Micro-gives.

A micro-give is any small act of generosity that costs little but carries weight.

It might be:

- Sending a quick note of encouragement.

- Commenting on someone's post with real thought.

- Forwarding a podcast episode or article that reminded you of them.

- Checking in on someone going through change.

- Congratulating a peer on their milestone sincerely, not strategically.

Micro-giving creates ripples.
They remind people of your character, not your circumstances.
And over time, those ripples reach back in ways you can't predict.

You don't have to be wealthy, powerful, or employed to give. You just have to be *aware*.

Generosity Is Your Growth Strategy

Generosity isn't about having extra, it's about noticing others.

It's quiet power saying, "I see you" and mean it.

Try This: The 5-Minute Give

Set a timer for five minutes and ask yourself:

- Who could use a little encouragement today?

- What could I share that might make someone's week easier or brighter?

Then do it immediately.

Send the message, share the resource, post the comment.

Five minutes a day builds more goodwill than five hours of self-promotion ever will.

Connectworking Challenge

This week, give something — your time, insight, or appreciation — without keeping score.
Expect nothing in return.
Then notice how it feels.

Generosity isn't just a growth strategy. It's a sanity strategy.
Because when you focus on giving, you stop worrying about what you're missing.
You remember what you already have and that's where confidence grows.

Next up: Kindness as a Competitive Advantage: How warmth, empathy, and genuine care set you apart.

Chapter 9

Kindness as a Competitive Advantage

How warmth, empathy, and genuine care set you apart.

Some people roll their eyes when they hear the word *kindness.*

They picture it as soft, sentimental, or even naïve; a nice thing to have, but not exactly a "business strategy."

They couldn't be more wrong.

Kindness is memorable.
Kindness is magnetic.

And in a noisy, competitive world, kindness is what makes you stand out.

Think about the people you still talk about years later: the boss who saw your potential before you did, the coworker who made time for you when no one else did, or the stranger who turned a bad day around.

They weren't always the smartest or most successful people in the room. But they left an impression that lasted because they made you *feel seen*.

> **Kindness is the trait people remember most.**

That's the real secret of connection.
You don't have to be impressive to be remembered.
You just have to be kind.

One of my clients, Dave, was interviewing for a senior role after being laid off from his company of fifteen years. He felt nervous and a little bitter. "I'm tired of pretending everything's fine," he told me.

Kindness as a Competitive Advantage

Before the interview, we practiced small grounding steps: slow his breathing, smile, and lead with curiosity instead of fear.

When the interviewer asked about his layoff, he decided not to gloss over the experience.
Dave said, "It was tough, but I learned a lot about empathy — for myself and others. There are so many people going through layoffs. I even started a weekly networking group to help myself and others stay connected."

The manager leaned forward and said quietly, "I came to this job after a layoff. I remember how challenging it was."
The whole tone of the interview changed.

He didn't get that job, but a month later, that same manager referred him to another company.
Because Dave didn't just talk about experience; he showed transparency.

Here's the thing: people can sense intention.
They know when you're genuinely interested and when you're just checking a box.
Kindness isn't a tactic; it's energy that people feel long after the conversation ends.

Being kind doesn't mean being a pushover. It means being grounded, compassionate, and respectful even when you're tired, disappointed, or scared.
It's strength with softness.

Science backs this up.
Studies show that warmth and competence together create the strongest impressions.
People trust those who combine skill with humanity, not just one or the other.
And when it comes to careers, people hire based on *trust*.

That's why kindness works. It signals reliability, humility, and emotional intelligence.
It makes people want to help you succeed, not out of obligation, but because it feels good to do so.

Try This: The 10-Second Pause

Before you send your next email, text, or message, pause for ten seconds and ask:

- How will this make the other person feel?
- Does it sound human, or hurried?
- Can I add one more ounce of kindness — a thank-you, a word of encouragement, a moment of warmth?

That tiny pause can change everything.

Because kindness, when intentional, is contagious.

Connectworking Challenge

This week, practice one act of deliberate kindness every day. Not random, but intentional.
> Send a note of appreciation.
> Listen without interrupting.
> Give credit where it's due.

No one remembers the person who networked the hardest.
They remember the one who made them feel like they mattered.

And that, my friend, is how kindness quietly wins.

Next up: Connection in the Digital Age: How to bring warmth to a world that runs on Wi-Fi.

Chapter 10

Connection in the Digital Age

How to bring warmth to a world that runs on Wi-Fi.

Technology has made it easier than ever to reach people and at the same time, harder than ever to *connect* with them.

You can message hundreds of people on LinkedIn, comment on posts, even attend virtual networking events from your kitchen table.

And yet, so many people still feel invisible.

That's because the digital world amplifies what already exists.

If you show up distracted, it multiplies.

If you show up authentic, that multiplies too.

The trick isn't to use more tools, it's to bring more *humanity* to them.

A client once told me, "I've sent out hundreds of LinkedIn messages, and nothing happens."
When I looked at her messages, I could see why. They were polite, polished, and completely forgettable.

She was following a formula:
"Hi, hope you're well. I'm reaching out to connect and learn more about your company."

Nice enough. But there was no *you* in it.

So, we rewrote it together.
"Hi, I've been following your work on employee well-being. That post about burnout really hit home. I've been there too. Would you be open to a short chat sometime?"

Same platform. Same person.
Different energy.

She got a reply within a few days.

Connection in the Digital Age

People respond to *tone* more than words.
You can feel warmth through a screen.
You can sense curiosity and sincerity.
It's not about punctuation or perfect grammar; it's about presence.

Digital connection isn't a numbers game. It's an energy game.
And your energy travels.

> **Show up human in a world that auto-replies.**

Here's what I advise my clients:
Show up online the same way you'd show up in person.
If you wouldn't say it to someone's face, don't post it.
If you would smile when you say it out loud, add that same warmth in writing.
If you'd listen attentively in person, don't scroll when someone else is speaking on a video call.

Small digital manners matter because they add up to big impressions.

You don't need to be a social media expert to connect online. You just need to be consistent, curious, and kind.

Here are three simple ways to make technology work *for* you:

1. **Voice over text.**
   When possible, send a short voice note instead of another typed message. The tone, laughter, and warmth can't be mistaken.

2. **Comments over likes.**
   Likes are quick; comments are connection.
   Add a sentence that shows you read and cared.

3. **Gratitude over goals.**
   Before posting or messaging, ask: *Am I trying to get something, or give something?*
   Gratitude always draws better responses than desperation.

Try This: The Human Filter

Before hitting send on any message, run it through this simple filter:

Would I talk this way if we were sitting across from each other?

If the answer is no, rewrite it until it sounds like *you*.

 Connectworking Challenge

Send one digital message today that sounds like your real voice.

It might be a comment, a DM, or a quick note.

Keep it warm, short, and human.

No buzzwords. No filler. Just you.

Because even in a digital world, connection is still human work.

Next up: The Quiet Connector: How introverts thrive at Connectworking — without pretending to be extroverts.

Introverts build **trust** without trying

Chapter 11

The Quiet Connector

How introverts thrive at Connectworking — without pretending to be extroverts.

If you've ever walked into a networking event, scanned the room, and immediately looked for the nearest exit, this chapter is for you.

Some people feed on crowds and conversation.
They walk in like the air just changed because they arrived.
You, on the other hand, might walk in and think, "Where can I stand that doesn't feel awkward?"

Let's start here: *there's nothing wrong with you.*
Introverts aren't bad at connection.
They're just bad at pretending to be extroverts.

One of my clients, Susan, used to describe herself as "socially allergic."

She hated mixers, dreaded Zoom icebreakers, and would rather clean her cat's litterbox than "network."

But she also wanted new opportunities, so she felt stuck.

I told her what I'll tell you: you don't have to change your personality to connect.

> **Introverts connect deeper, not louder.**

You just have to connect *your way*.

So, she did.

Instead of big events, she invited one person a week for coffee at a new shop.

No pitch, no pressure, no forced small talk, just curiosity and connection.

And guess what? Those quiet, one-on-one conversations became her signature strength.

Within six months, she'd built stronger relationships than years of trying to "work the room."

Her calm, thoughtful energy became her brand.

The Quiet Connector

That's the power of being a *Quiet Connector*.

Introverts often make the best Connectworkers because they naturally do what most people forget to do — *listen*.
They notice details and ask real questions. They make others feel heard.

Quiet curiosity is magnetic in a world full of people trying to impress.
When you're comfortable in the pause, people lean in.

But connection still takes energy, and introverts need to manage that intentionally.
It's not about *avoiding* people, it's about balancing output and input. Here's how:

1. **Honor your rhythm.**

    Plan connection moments around your natural energy. If mornings drain you, schedule calls in the afternoon. If crowds feel heavy, focus on smaller settings.
    Energy management is not selfish; it's strategy.

2. **Use preparation as confidence.**

    Introverts often shine when they feel ready. Do a little homework: read someone's post, review their background, jot down a question. That prep gives you an anchor when the nerves start whispering.

3. **Redefine visibility.**

    You don't have to post daily selfies or host webinars.
    Instead, comment thoughtfully or share an article with your perspective.
    Show up consistently in ways that feel natural. That's enough.

4. **Create recharge rituals.**

    After connecting, give yourself quiet time to refill.
    Walk your dog. Listen to music. Step outside. Recovery isn't avoidance, it's maintenance.

Try This: The Three Conversations Rule

When attending any event, whether it's online or in person, aim for three *meaningful* interactions.
That's it. No more, no less.
You don't need to meet thirty people; you need three genuine connections.
Quality beats quantity every time.

Write down their names and a detail or two about each conversation.
Follow up with a short note:

"I really enjoyed our chat about [topic]. Thanks for making that event feel comfortable."

That's how introverts win — with warmth.

> **Connectworking Challenge**
>
> Make your **Connection Menu.**
>
> List three simple, low-stress ways you'll connect this month.
>
> Maybe it's:
>
> > One coffee with a friend.
>
> > One thoughtful comment online.
>
> > One "just checking in" message.
>
> Then stop apologizing for being quiet.
> Quiet doesn't mean unseen; it means intentional.
>
> Your calm energy makes people feel safe and that's what true connection needs most.

Next up: When It Doesn't Click: How to handle silence, rejection, and mismatched energy with grace.

Chapter 12

When It Doesn't Click

How to handle silence, rejection, and mismatched energy with grace.

Not every connection will click.
Not every conversation will flow.
And not everyone will respond, no matter how kind or thoughtful your outreach was.

It's one of the hardest lessons in connection… and one of the most freeing once you learn it.

Because when you stop expecting every spark to turn into a fire, you start enjoying the warmth of the ones that do.

A client once shared with me, "I must be terrible at networking. People just don't reply."
She'd been sending messages for weeks. Half of her notes of encouragement, small introductions, even thank-you messages after interviews went unanswered.

When we looked closer, it wasn't that she was doing anything wrong.
It's that people were busy. Distracted. Overwhelmed. Her messages were lovely, but sometimes timing and attention are tricky things in a noisy world.

That silence wasn't rejection. It was *life*.

We've been conditioned to take every non-response personally.
But the truth is, most of the time it has nothing to do with us.
People are juggling work, family, and their own anxieties.
Sometimes your message lands during someone's family emergency and your message simply fell to the bottom of the priority pile. It happens to us all.

When It Doesn't Click

The key is not to close your heart every time it happens.

Because connection requires resilience and the courage to keep showing up, even when the response isn't what you hoped for.

> **Rejection is redirection. Trust the reroute.**

Here's something to remember: silence doesn't equal failure.
Sometimes it's just space.
And space gives both sides room to grow.

When someone doesn't respond, you can still wish them well and keep your energy moving forward.

You never know who might circle back later.
I've seen it happen countless times: a message ignored months ago suddenly leads to a reconnection, an apology, or even an opportunity.

People return when they're ready.
Your job is to stay ready, not resentful.

If you're struggling with that quiet, try this:
Instead of asking, "Why didn't they respond?"
Ask, "What did I learn from reaching out?"

You might realize you practiced vulnerability.
You might see that you showed consistency.
Or that you followed through on your word.

Those wins strengthen your connection muscles.

Try This: The "Grace File"

Create a folder or note on your phone called *Grace*. Each time something doesn't click, such as a message that was ignored, a meeting that fizzled, or a rejection that stings, write down one sentence about what you learned from it.

- Maybe it's "I handled that with kindness."

- Maybe it's "I reached out even when I was nervous."

- Maybe it's just "I showed up."

Then move on. You've already won the part that matters.

When It Doesn't Click

> **Connectworking Challenge**
>
> Reach out to someone again, even if the last time went nowhere.
>
> Not to follow up, but to reconnect with no expectation. Also, never forward the prior message pointing out
>
> they failed to respond earlier.
>
> Keep it light. Keep it warm.
>
> "Just thought of you today and wanted to say hello."
>
> If it clicks this time, great. If not, you still practiced the art of staying open.
>
> Because real connection isn't measured by who responds, it's measured by who you become when you keep trying.

Next up: The Ripple Effect: How small acts of connection create waves that reach further than you'll ever know.

Today's **actions** create lasting **impact**

Chapter 13

The Ripple Effect

How small acts of connection create waves that reach further than you'll ever know.

One of my favorite parts of this work is watching people realize how far their kindness travels. Sometimes it's immediate, like a message that turns into a coffee chat that turns into a job.
Other times, it takes months or even years before the ripple circles back.

But it always does.

Connection never disappears.
It moves quietly through conversations, introductions, and the way you made someone feel.
It becomes part of their story and yours.

A client once told me about a woman she'd met years earlier at a volunteer event. They'd had a single, light conversation about travel and midlife pivots, but had no contact since.

Out of nowhere, that woman reached out on LinkedIn:

"You probably don't remember me, but you said something that stuck with me. You told me I wasn't too old to start over. That gave me the courage to go back to school. I finished my degree and now am the head of a research team. We're expanding and you were the first person I thought of. Would you be interested in learning about it?"

She wasn't exaggerating. That one simple conversation shared while helping others changed her path.

That's the ripple effect.
You never know which moment will matter to someone else.

The Ripple Effect

We often think our words and gestures vanish once the conversation ends.
But they don't.
They land somewhere, sometimes quietly, sometimes powerfully.

> **Your smallest kindness may be someone's turning point.**

Your comment might give someone courage.
Your message might remind someone they're not alone.
Your example might inspire them to take their own small step.

And when they do, *they* create ripples too.

That's how human connection grows, not through grand gestures, but through everyday grace.

The beauty of *Connectworking* is that it asks nothing more than this:
Be human. Be curious. Be kind. Be consistent.

Every conversation, every message, every quiet act of generosity contributes to a bigger current; one that keeps moving even when you can't see it.

That's the magic of connection.

You start by helping one person, and somehow, you help yourself too.

Try This: The Gratitude Map

Draw a quick map with your name in the center.
Then, around it, jot down the people who've helped, inspired, or encouraged you in the last year.
Now add one line connecting each name to a person *you* have encouraged, helped, or introduced.

That's your ripple and visible proof that you've been making a difference all along.

Connectworking Challenge

This week, reach out to one person who once helped or encouraged you — even in a small way.
Tell them what their kindness meant to you.
That's how ripples become waves.

Because connection doesn't end when the moment does.
It lives on, carried forward by every person who felt your light.

Next up: The Human Advantage in an AI World: How to stay human when technology does the talking.

STOP NETWORKING... START CONNECTWORKING®

Humanity
beats
algorithm

Chapter 14

The Human Advantage in an AI World

How to stay human when technology does the talking.

I'm often on the receiving end of networking requests in the form of emails and direct messages from people who want advice, insight, a connection, or sometimes just a quick reply. I read a lot of them. Increasingly, messages land in my inbox that look perfect.
The grammar is polished, the tone is friendly, and the request is clear.

But something about it feels off.
It isn't *bad*, it just doesn't sound like a human who genuinely wants to connect.

And that's when I know:
I'm not reading a message from a person.
I'm reading a message crafted by AI... technically flawless, but emotionally empty.

And that's what's quietly happening all around us: conversations are being replaced by content.

Technology is evolving fast.
AI writes résumés, drafts messages, and even helps us "network" — if by that we mean sending a stream of perfect but personality-free messages into the void.

But here's the truth: connection can't be automated.

You can outsource your words, but you can't outsource your warmth.
You can use tools to save time, but not to build trust.
Because trust doesn't come from efficiency, it comes from empathy.

The Human Advantage in an AI World

Artificial intelligence can be an incredible ally.
It can help you brainstorm, summarize, and refine.
It can help you *reach* more people.

But only you can help people *feel* something.

In a world of prompts, be the person.

When you show up as yourself, with all your slightly messy and wonderfully human qualities, that's what stands out in a world of digital polish.

So instead of fearing AI, learn to use it wisely.
Think of it as your assistant, not your replacement.

Let it organize your ideas, but don't let it speak for you.
Let it help you prepare, but don't let it pretend to care.

Connection is still a full-contact, human sport.

A client named Christina found a better way.

She was preparing for a final interview with the CEO of a company she admired. Instead of using AI to generate another batch of "perfect" answers, she used it differently: for *research.*

Christina asked AI to help her learn more about the company's leadership.
Within minutes, she learned that the CEO was an avid runner who had completed the Chicago Marathon.

As it happened, Christina had run that same race just a few months before.

During the interview, when the CEO asked what motivated her outside of work, Christina mentioned her love of running, and her experience at the Chicago Marathon.
The CEO's face lit up immediately.

"You ran Chicago too? I *loved* that one!"

And just like that, the energy in the room shifted.

Two professionals became two people.
A simple shared experience found through technology and expressed through humanity built instant connection.

Christina didn't use AI to fake connection.
She used it to *find* connection.
That's a significant difference.

The Three Rules of Human Connection in a Digital Age

1. **Draft, Don't Delegate.**
   Use AI to get started, but never to finish.
   Let it help you brainstorm or organize, then make the words your own. Add humor, empathy, or detail that only you could know.

2. **Be the Filter, Not the Follower.**
   Don't let technology decide how you sound. Before sending anything, ask: "Would I say this to a friend?" If not, rewrite until it feels natural.

3. **Remember the 90/10 Rule.**
   Let AI handle the 10% of busywork so you can spend 90% of your energy on what matters most; the human follow-through.

The irony is, the more advanced technology becomes, the more valuable our humanity becomes.

When everyone sounds perfect, sincerity becomes priceless.

When everyone automates, empathy becomes your edge.

That's the human advantage; it's the one thing no algorithm can duplicate.

Your presence.

Your curiosity.

Your willingness to care.

That's what people remember.

Try This: Would I Say This to Myself?

Take one message you've written with AI, maybe a LinkedIn note, thank-you email, or outreach draft, and rewrite it in your own words.

Read both versions out loud.

Which one sounds like a conversation you'd want to have?

Connectworking Challenge

This week, choose one situation where you'd normally use technology and replace it with a human moment.

Pick up the phone. Send a voice note. Ask one deeper question.

Because in a world where technology can mimic almost anything, being *human* is now your greatest differentiator.

Next up: The Moment You Know It's Working: Connection changes everything... including you.

Congratulations! you're Connectworking!

The Moment You Know It's Working

Connection changes everything... including you.

There isn't a single "aha" moment when you realize Connectworking is working.

It happens quietly.

You'll notice it one morning when your inbox feels less like a to-do list and more like a conversation. When people you haven't met yet feel familiar. When opportunities find you, not because you chased them, but because you showed up long enough for someone to see you.

That's the shift.
It's not louder, it's lighter.
You stop trying so hard to *network* and start living connected.

One of my clients described it perfectly.

He said, "I didn't notice how much I'd changed until someone asked me what I'd been doing to meet so many good people lately. I told them that I stopped looking for the right contacts and started being the right kind of person."

That's it.

That's the essence of it all.

When you lead with authenticity, curiosity, and kindness, connection becomes effortless.

And when connection becomes effortless, opportunities grow naturally.

There's something freeing about realizing your worth isn't tied to your title, your job, or your LinkedIn headline.

It's tied to how you make people feel.

How you listen, and how you show up when no one's watching.

That's the power of real connection that gives back more than it takes.

The Moment You Know It's Working

So, if you're reading this and wondering where to start, don't overthink it.

Start small.
Start kind.
Start today.

Send the text.
Write the thank-you.
Ask the question.
Give the compliment.

> **Connection changes everything— starting with you.**

And trust that every one of those small acts is a ripple in motion.
Because connection doesn't end with a conversation, it expands with every person you impact.

You don't need to "network" anymore.
You just need to keep being real.
Keep being curious.
Keep being you.

That's when you'll know it's working.

Final Reflection

> "The shortest distance between two people is honesty. The lasting bond is kindness."

Let that be your north star, in your career, in your community, and in your life.

You were never meant to collect contacts.

You were meant to create connection.

Conversation Prompts

Your next great conversation starts here

STOP NETWORKING... START CONNECTWORKING®

Conversation Prompts for Job Seekers

1. "What's something you're working on that you're excited about?"

2. "What's the best career advice you've ever ignored—but later realized was true?"

3. "What's one challenge in your industry that more people should be talking about?"

4. "I'm curious—what skills do you think will matter most in the next few years?"

5. "What's something you learned the hard way that you wish you'd known sooner?"

6. "If someone were entering your field today, what would you tell them to focus on?"

7. "What skills or habits have helped you thrive in your role?"

Conversation Prompts for Introverts

1. "I overheard you mention ____. I'd love to hear more about that."
2. "I'm challenging myself to meet one new person today. Mind if it's you?"
3. "I'm exploring what's next—what lights you up in your role?"
4. "What's the most interesting challenge on your plate this month?"
5. "What helps you stay motivated when things get messy?"
6. "If you were starting your career today, what would you do differently?"
7. "What's a great piece of advice you got that actually worked?"

Conversation Prompts for Follow-Through

1. "I really enjoyed our conversation. I'm still thinking about what you said about ____."

2. "You mentioned ____; here's the article/resource you inspired me to find."

3. "Loved your insight on ____. How did that project turn out?"

4. "You gave me great advice—I actually tried it!"

5. "Let me know if there's a way I can support what you're building."

6. "You mentioned wanting to learn about ____. Here's something that might be helpful."

7. "How did your meeting/interview/presentation go?"

Conversation Prompts for LinkedIn Messages

1. "I'm exploring new directions and your perspective stood out."

2. "Your comment on _____ was so refreshing. What inspired it?"

3. "Your career pivot is fascinating—can I ask what sparked it?"

4. "I noticed we share a passion for _____. What's your story there?"

5. "Loved your insight on _____—do you talk about that anywhere else?"

6. "I'm making bold career moves—your story gave me a nudge."

7. "Your take on ___ was spot-on. I'm curious; what's your background there?"

Conversation Prompts for Continuing the Conversation

1. "I'm glad we met—mind if I stay in touch?"

2. "Thanks for the conversation—let me know how I can support you."

3. "I'd love to hear how ____ turns out. Keep me posted?"

4. "This was fun—let's do it again."

5. "Feel free to reach out anytime—door's open."

6. "You've given me so much to think about—can we chat again soon?"

7. "I'm grateful we met—hope this isn't the last time we talk."

Share your favorite conversation prompts.
#connectworking

Bonus

Connectworking® 30-Day Practice

Welcome to your 30-Day Connectworking Practice; a month of small, meaningful actions that bring more humanity into your life. Each day offers a bite-sized challenge to spark curiosity, courage, and kindness.

Download the Connectworking 30-Day Challenge Workbook at www.iamjenfort.com/resources.

Create Your Intention:

Before you begin, finish this sentence:
"Over the next 30 days, I want to show up as someone who..."

_____

_____

_____

If you're stuck, here are a few examples:

"*Over the next 30 days, I want to show up as someone who sprinkles encouragement everywhere I go — a high-five here, a 'you've got this!' there. I'm choosing to be the person whose energy lifts rooms.*"

"*Over the next 30 days, I want to show up as someone who listens deeply, engages thoughtfully, and builds trust through my presence.*"

"*Over the next 30 days, I want to show up as someone who doesn't force small talk, but instead seeks one real, meaningful conversation at a time. Depth over volume is my superpower.*"

Week 1: Reconnect with Your Real Self

Goal: *Build self-awareness, clarity, and authentic confidence.*

Day	Prompt	Done
1	Write three words describing how you want people to feel after meeting you.	
2	Reframe one fear about networking into a new belief.	
3	Give a genuine compliment on someone's effort or character	
4	List 10 people who've positively impacted your life.	
5	Send a gratitude message to one of them.	
6	Post something real (not perfect) on social media.	
7	Reflect: What surprised you this week?	

Week 2: Reach Out and Reconnect

Goal: *Reignite dormant connections through small, intentional moments.*

Day	Prompt	Done
8	Message someone you haven't spoken to in a year.	
9	Leave a thoughtful comment online.	
10	Record and send a 20-second voice or video note.	
11	Introduce two people who you think should meet.	
12	Ask someone what they're working on, then listen.	
13	Share a resource or recommendation.	
14	Reflect: How did these reconnections feel?	

Week 3: Radiate Generosity

Goal: Lead with giving, not getting.

Day	Prompt	Done
15	Thank someone who rarely gets thanked.	
16	Offer help with no strings attached.	
17	Spotlight someone else's success.	
18	Schedule a "just because" coffee.	
19	Write a LinkedIn recommendation.	
20	Encourage one person today.	
21	Reflect: What did generosity shift in you?	

Week 4: Grow Your Ripple

Goal: Turn consistency into community.

Day	Prompt	Done
22	Host a 20-minute "catch-up coffee."	
23	Join a new group that aligns with your values.	
24	Share a vulnerable or growth story.	
25	Follow up with someone new this month.	
26	Ask, "How can I support you right now?"	
27	Create your Friday "gratitude ritual."	
28	Reflect: What's changing in how you connect?	

Connectworking® 30-Day Practice

Week 5: Make It a Movement

Goal: Integrate Connectworking habits for life.

Day	Prompt	Done
29	Choose three habits to continue weekly.	
30	Write a Connectworking Manifesto *"From now on, I will…"*	

Closing Reflections

Now that you've completed the 30-day practice, ask yourself these two questions:
What changed in how you see yourself?
What changed in how others responded to you?

_____
_____
_____
_____
_____
_____
_____
_____
_____

Connectworking®
© 2025 JAC Your Life LLC | All rights reserved.
www.iamjenfort.com | #Connectworking

Thank you!

Thank you for reading this book and bringing Connectworking into your world in whatever way feels right for you.

Please take a moment and scan below to leave a review on Amazon. I read each one, and your feedback helps shape the future of Connectworking.

And, if this book sparked an insight or shifted how you connect, I'd love for you to share your story using #Connectworking.

Thank you again for your support.

Acknowledgments

No one writes a book about connection alone.
To my clients, friends, and fellow travelers who trusted me with your stories, thank you for sharing. You constantly teach me that real connection is never a strategy; it's a way of being.

To Clive, you are my favorite connection of all.

To Margaret and Mark, you are true examples of how purpose-based connection can produce amazing results. I thank you both for believing in my ideas and helping bring them to life.

Stay connected by joining the community on social media using **#Connectworking** and follow @iamjenfort and @wisdomandwarnings

About the Author

Jen Fort is a writer, speaker, and career transition coach who believes connection is the heartbeat of every career and every story. After an unexpected departure ended her twenty-year corporate career, she turned that detour into purpose, helping thousands of people rediscover confidence, curiosity, and meaning on the other side of change.

Jen is the creator of **Connectworking**® and the **Wisdom & Warnings**® series, collections of real-world advice drawn from life's pivotal moments. Her work blends humor, humanity, and hope, reminding readers that success isn't about collecting contacts but creating conversations that matter.

When she's not coaching, writing or speaking, Jen's adventuring outdoors with her husband, Clive, proving that the best connections often start with curiosity and leave you with a good story.

www.ingramcontent.com/pod-product-compliance
Lightning Source LLC
Chambersburg PA
CBHW060512030426
42337CB00015B/1869